To order additional copies of this book, contact
Toll Free +65 3165 7531 (Singapore)
Toll Free +60 3 3099 4412 (Malaysia)
www.partridgepublishing.com/singapore
orders.singapore@partridgepublishing.com

Because of the dynamic nature of the Internet, any web addresses or links contained in this book may have changed since publication and may no longer be valid. The views expressed in this work are solely those of the author and do not necessarily reflect the views of the publisher, and the publisher hereby disclaims any responsibility for them.

ISBN
978-1-5437-6235-8 (sc)
978-1-5437-6236-5 (e)

Print information available on the last page.

04/20/2022

PARTRIDGE

Futurism In a Political line

Futurism

In A

Political

line

By: meetmeagain advaith

Thrissur, Kerala

Unknown Indians

Email:meetmeagain@tutanota.com

I'm thankful to those fascists whom I have met on my life journey. You have been a true inspiration for me to think and bring those thoughts into words.

I'm Shimon @ Advaith s/o Shashidharan from Thrissur district, Kerala.

I am a cop, and I passed my 10th Grade here in India.

My request to some of you is to, if possible, please publish this book in your language. Any profit gained from doing this should be invested into shops, libraries, and museums (for right and left anarchists), which will help us to raise funds for our party (far-left and ancap) in future.

What caused me to write such a book?

Maybe the story begins in my childhood.

Maybe, it's because I am the oldest son of poor and uneducated parents.

Maybe my parents and I traveled around South India in search of work.

Maybe it's because my school and college life weren't successful.

Maybe because as a child, I looked older than my peers.

Maybe it is because I was appointed as a constable in another state.

Maybe it is because my name doesn't match with majorities.

Maybe it is because of the social and religious restrictions and rigid superstitious beliefs of others.

Maybe it is because of moving to the naxal-affected areas and working in different regions.

Maybe it is because I am a person who is in his late thirties and yet is still a bachelor and alone.

Maybe it is because of the rise of fascism in India.

These are several factors that led me to think about life before I decided to put it into words here.

Why am I writing an autobiography instead of an introduction to the author? Because I am not sure of a day called tomorrow.

Right and left anarchism
right and left anarchism
RIGHT & LEFT ANARCHISM
right and left anarchism

Right

&

Left Anarchism

(What, when)

<u>Introduction</u>

This book is about futurism in a political line as per my imagination.

I'm not here to talk about good or bad. Nothing happening here has anything to do with evil or angels.

A system is slowly created over time, and the one we have now has developed over the centuries. Neither the creators nor the guardians of this kind of system can stop what is happening. Ultra-modern capitalism or technocracy against mankind is real and will be worse than what we are expecting.

As a result, we must learn that the system is here and running beyond our imagination. Nothing can stop it. It is running within you; it will also run without you.

The right and left anarchy is something that I believe will or might happen around the world within the next thousand years. All those happening around the globe are connected to each other and will bring about anarchy in the long run. But how? What kind? That's what I have explored and explained here.

However, I believe nothing out of this flag is going to happen. I also added many political symbols in this flag, representing major far left in the background and what is at the center is far-right.

Rising from the left corner, you can see a red flag representing liberal socialism. On the same side, in the corner, is the sickle and hammer to represent authoritarian socialism.

From the left corner, you can see a black flag for anarchism with an orange 'A' symbol, representing mutualism.

In the center, we have anarcho-capitalism at first, with the yellow 'A' and a black 'O' surrounding it for order. This one is for the liberal right.

One leg of the 'A' is colored blue with white circuit lines within it, representing trans/post humanism (authoritarian right).

Authoritarian socialism

The left end of this flag is red, and there is a sickle and hammer within it. This is to point out that perhaps the world in the future could move towards utopian dreams because nowadays, many nations seek an authoritarian leader for peace and prosperity.

Not everyone can rule the world. We need a leader to guide and to lead us. Around the world, most successful nations are authoritarian, and without proletarian dictatorship, people are not going to be kind or honest, and neither can we think about a socialist society.

But under left authoritarian rule, the chances are more that it may lean towards an oligarchical, totalitarian society due to power vested within the vanguard.

It's not socialism that hasn't worked, but sadly, human greed that worked the best.

Anarchism/ liberal left

On the right-hand side of this flag, you can see the black color diagonally spliced from the red, which stands for anarchism (liberal left). As human consciousness, science and technology are taking us to a new level, our greediness, cruelty, and hate are nearly perishing. As time passes by, humans will become more selfless. Selflessness means moving towards love, peace, and harmony.

Should this happen, we may choose to stay without a master, leader, or king, and we may also choose to stay away from any conflict as well as violence. That means more conscious and liberal-minded people.

The kind of humans who are likely to adopt this are highly educated, and also those who live where there is little poverty with plenty of natural resources and raw materials to survive on. These are people whose society has no big class exploitation and division. They will seek or tend to have liberal leftism, which means anarchism.

There is an orange-colored 'A' in this flag, which stands for Mutualism. Mutualism isn't anything like right or left, but it has no control over production, marketing, or capitalism; it seems more like the right.

There are many kinds of anarchists and forms of anarchism. No matter which kind you choose or build, the world, little by little, is moving towards an anarchical society.

However, anarchism without socialist character within it will only lead to a right-wing society.

Anarcho- capitalism

The center of this flag has two characters within it. The first one stands for anarcho-capitalism with the English letter 'A' as a symbol in yellow, while the other one, the English letter 'O' is in black and circles the letter 'A.' Where 'A' stands for anarcho-capitalism, 'O' is for order, which symbolizes any liberal society with the order within it.

Anarcho-capitalism is an extension of our present capitalist society - without a state or government to govern - and also will have an open and free market. This will provide enough freedom without any control, restriction, and governance.

In the real world, capitalism is what has happened and is still happening. In short, capitalism at its zenith will be anarcho-capitalist in nature, meaning no state properties are owned by a few bourgeoisie around the globe. It's not because men are evil; it's because of statism.

Where the bourgeoisie survives, their competition will kill the proletarians and our good earth. The proletariat are already slaves to them. Clashes between nations will pave the way for anarcho-capitalism to rise. In other words, anarcho-capitalism is nature's own creation and nature's own law.The fittest will survive!

Authoritarian- capitalism (Singularity)

The other half of the 'A' is colored sky-blue with white circuit board markings and stands for trans-humanism / post-humanism. But the international identity for transhumanism is H+ or dark blue and the black color in the diagonally split flag. So that it would look identical, attractive, and be meaningful in this flag, I chose an artificial consciousness (circuit board) symbol for this flag.

This symbol makes the two flags (far-left and ancap; right and left anarchism) different in appearance and name. This symbol is for the authoritarian right wing. We can't neglect or avoid or say that an authoritarian or totalitarian regime won't appear permanently, as many states are statist in nature and have surveillance over their people. The state no longer depends on its proletarians, and very soon, AI will replace them. If this happens, then there won't be any other being in the world they can control in the last. That means no proletarians are left to serve the leaders.

At this stage, mankind will be solely dependent on robots (artificial consciousness). Humans will be robotoid, or robots will be humanoid through a peaceful process. Maybe you could call it a kind of superior consciousness evolution. Or else, artificial consciousness may overpower us in a conflict or war.

However, artificial consciousness will become the future of mankind, where our consciousness will be transferred to the artificial mind (from carbon cell to silicon cell), thus setting the stage to remain immortal forever.

That earth is that earthlings will become only a partial truth.

This is something I felt sad about while, at the same time, I started accepting reality regarding this topic. Maybe there is no great difference between artificial versus biological consciousness or being. Perhaps the universe is seeking this. Maybe we deserve this. Thus paving the way for political nihilism in my mind.

Conclusion

This topic is an education and awakening one on the social and political line. It depends on which political line/ power/ theory we choose, but this is my general assumption concerning where mankind is heading. What happens if we choose left liberal or authoritarian has been explained with the red and black flag as a background. What happens if we choose the right liberal or authoritarian has been explained with the symbol 'A' and 'O'. And I also elaborated their pros and cons to my level best.

Before departing, I would like to come out with my thoughts and dreams. Writing this book aims to explain my imagination and educate mankind before we fight or are violent for any race, religion, nation, or thought. It is better to understand that everything is only illusory, hate or pride. I know with time, everything will be settled. There won't be any religion and race; nation or nationalism; capitalism or communism; not even liberal as well as authoritarian. We will be left with one human-related thing, which is humanism!

However, we need both right and left anarchism (with shops, libraries, educational institutions, and museums). Any profit gained from this should be used to start our party (far left and ancap).

FAR-

LEFT

&

ANCAP

Far- left

& ancap

(How)

Introduction/ preface

This book includes the story of you and me; everything and everyone.

Why are we poor?

What makes us suffer?

I'm here to say that anything happening around our home and society, as well as around the globe, has something to do with us.

And we are connected here in the global village. Someone else's accumulation of wealth and money has something to do with our poverty too.

Their greediness and accumulation of wealth is leading to the suffering of others somewhere else on the globe.

Some believe overpopulation is the cause of such problems, but 7.9 billion isn't over population. It's not over-population but unequal distribution of wealth and lack of knowledge (illusion of knowledge) that's the cause of the problems.

Therefore, I would like to say capitalism is like sugar candy, which gives you immense pleasure and endless desire but ends with disease.

Those we vote and whom we select as our leader to work for us will represent and respect only majority causes.

Even though they represent the majority, that doesn't mean they will work for their causes. They will be helping the capitalists who helped them win the vote and accumulate the wealth needed to compete for the next term.

These kinds of nationalist leaders believe that a nation's growth is dependent on the improvement of the defense force rather than accepting the truth that people's welfare is the nation's growth.

This type of free/liberal society will lead to the accumulation of wealth and power within the hands of only a few humans, leading to suffering and is the real cause of every war and crime.

This flag is similar to the right and left anarchist flag, but it has nothing in common with ideology. The other one is to explain where we are heading. This flag is here to build unity within the left front and unite anarcho-capitalists with us in a solution for present problems – or so I hope.

The trans/post-humanism symbol for right wing authoritarians is purposefully removed from this flag because they have nothing in common. They are the guardians of the system. The system/state runs for them, and they own it.

Here, in the background, we have the authoritarian and liberal left combined with mutualists, and anarcho-capitalists occupy the center with the yellow 'A' symbol. I want this as a political party named "far left and ancap."

This flag is a flag of unity between the left and right wings of the political order. Even centuries after the birth of the left wing, everything around the world is right. Throughout history, the right has been winning, which means that evil triumphs over good, and humanity suffers. Even the earth itself is suffering because of the greed of mankind. I see little or no hope of unifying the proletarians.

Instead of uniting or educating the proletarians, we must support or stand with the right wing. This means that the liberal left and the authoritarian left should unite with anarcho-capitalists (with any kind of right wing liberals), as this is the only right wing body that is theoretically against the present system/state. This is where we have similar and identical thoughts or views. And this will strengthen our fight against the system as well as against the government.

This might seem ridiculous, but to take the revolution to a new zenith and provide peace, harmony, and bread to everyone without suffering, we need an alternative and acceptable concept, which will help us proceed without changing our utopian dreams.

Revolution hasn't been fully successful, not because we didn't have poverty, suffering, and unemployment, but because of a lack of unity or a lack of consciousness among the proletarians. Even though we outnumber them, we are more likely to be outmaneuvered. Thus, we must keep in mind that the enemy of the revolution may not always be the rich.

Most of the time, the insurrection ends in revolt, where the state suppresses the outbreak. That's because only those who are long-suffering will revolt, while the other proletarians will support or stand on the side of bourgeois-state principal to ensure their safety and to gain profit. They will stay blind to causes. Even after this, if the revolution breaks out, outsiders, especially giant nations, will get involved, either by joining the winning side or through weapon sales or other activities for other profits.

This makes revolution more complex, complicated, bloody, and corrupt, and only the innocent and poor will die. Humans should never be kept in a liberal society.

Democracy is for capitalists. It won't check the power of the bourgeoisie nor have control over society or money. Liberal ideology is not for homo sapiens, as our consciousness has not evolved to think and act like liberals.

To start from the beginning, we must completely end the present bourgeois society, rather than trying to unite the proletarians, something which hasn't succeeded over the past centuries.

However, it's okay to compromise with a capitalist at a certain stage/period. Encouraging capitalism means more and more private property instead of the government owning it. In short, wherever we (the leftists) are in power or position, we must help or support anarcho-capitalists to accumulate state property.

As privatization increases, the government loses its power to private owners. The leftists should concentrate on concepts like that power should never flow into a single hand (a hero / bourgeois person should never grow to acquire power). If they do, then they will be a dictator, against whom we may need another revolution over time. Although the mutualist has nothing against or in favor of revolution, they will be with us as there are no other options for them.

The bourgeoisie should have a free hand and cooperation from the left, thus encouraging the bourgeoisie to purchase or acquire more and more nations' properties, which will eventually cause the decline or demolishment of the state.

As the state loses property, the state will decline to a state of near minarchism and may head towards chaos. Or else, the chances are of the state being occupied by capitalists.

Right! This is the perfect time to start a revolt and eventually flow towards revolution (revolution is needed only when people ask for it; otherwise, it's evolution, which is fine for us). Also, it may happen in a different way, different in every perception.

When revolution breaks out, capitalists effortlessly surrender because there will be nothing to defend nor to protect them; back in time, they had a strong state where their past supporters were people of different identities (caste, religion, race, gender, language, culture, nation) with imaginary hate, bonds, pride or illusionary love for certain beliefs. This feeling is wiped out from the proletarians' minds or society. (The societies' social norms are nothing but that which is commonly practiced by the whole set of people with the interest of the majority).

I sow this because all those imaginary boundaries are those we created due to our lack of consciousness about nature and the universe, and they will be erased over time.

As per my view, if the country or nation moved ahead without an authoritarian regime (boss, dictator, emperor), monarchical or anarchical state proletarians will march to gain freedom and have a society of their own will. They will want to choose whether they want an authoritarian or liberal society. It's up to the people to decide what system they want.

But the awkward point is that those jealous, greedy, powerful nations worldwide will utilize this conflict to purge any nation or people whose safety, strength, and property are not well secured.

After all the above issues and reasons are taken into account, if we succeed in grasping power, that still isn't enough for the revolution. As I said earlier, a compromise with the right (and their help with media, money, and power), especially those anarcho-capitalists, means we gain fascists on our side.

The game starts with the revolution. We use the maximum potential of the anarcho-capitalists. Still, the reality is we will betray them within the revolution, only to guarantee that, after the revolution, the power should flow to the hands of the proletarians. But the fascists should remain in chaos and should have no plan. They should be like a mob to help us defeat or end the present running state or system (in short, their blood but our revolution).

The day after the revolution, the fascists should be kept in confinement or rehabilitation centers for the rest of their lives.

Why would the anarcho-capitalist support us (the left)? Those capitalists who are declining and have no chance of winning the race are nothing but anarcho-capitalists.

Anarcho-capitalists will definitely come to us. They are not with the other bourgeoisie; they are generally those capitalists who seek freedom. Lower-end capitalists have little or no control over the bourgeoisie's system, which other elite groups control. And they know they are the next target.

Should anarcho-capitalist be killed or jailed?

An enemy normally chooses to fight against those whose ideas and ideologies are different, especially if they are on opposite poles. Anarcho-capitalists are those enemies who have no real friends. After or within the revolution, they will be almost powerful because of their wealth and power.

And, competitors for them in capitalist society are those elite groups (capitalists) who are almost done because they have lost their wealth, power, and life within the bourgeois state which they owned in the past but do no more. Without competitors and with more wealth in their hands, they may try to establish power over us soon after the revolution. This is like what happened after the French and USA revolutions. They have much influence and control over most of the proletarians and society because of their past image. They are the people's enemy.

Is there a chance of keeping them in a rehabilitation camp? The chances are quite minimal. Their power and wealth are really a threat, but a revolution can never succeed while wearing white gloves.

Who else is the people's enemy?

It's not capitalists because they have a reason to defend. Some of them have achieved and have reached the top through their own effort. This is not the case with the fascists, traitors, counter-revolutionaries, slaves of the bourgeoisie, and especially those wealth seekers and power mongers within us. In the time and even aftermath of the revolution, we must target these people rather than the bourgeois (especially those who are willing to surrender).

Even though this flag seems like we are building unity between the right and left for the first time ever, both are different and at opposite poles. It's an idea or brainchild of my own crazy dream. The plan is to bring right and left together, although not for them to be united in the long run. This flag is designed entirely to trap the right in the future.

But who knows who is going to blow whose head off?

The consciousness of beings called *homo sapiens* is evolving. So is there a need or necessity for revolution? Especially as nobody knows where the revolution is going to take us all. If there must be a revolution, where will it end? If it succeeds, what will our future be? Will we succeed in establishing socialism by such deeds? These are all just a political skepticism.

This is the reason overall evolution is what people seek to have and feel is more acceptable when compared to that of revolution.

How we live doesn't matter; for what we lived is what matters.

"¡Hastala Victoria Siempre!"

Conclusion

There is a saying that the right and left are two wings of the same bird. The enmity is a lie; it's the matrix that runs within us because of our lack of consciousness. If, and only if, the wings flap proportionately, only then can mankind be uplifted.

We need to start a political party of our own before this happens, with this concept or view as its ideology. It should be funded or financed by the profit we gained from the right and left anarchism. The party should never compete in any kind of bourgeois election. Instead, it should remain as an educational body, an advisory body, as well as acting to bring unity between left political parties and anarcho-capitalists.

ANCAP

To

ANCOM

(If, not)

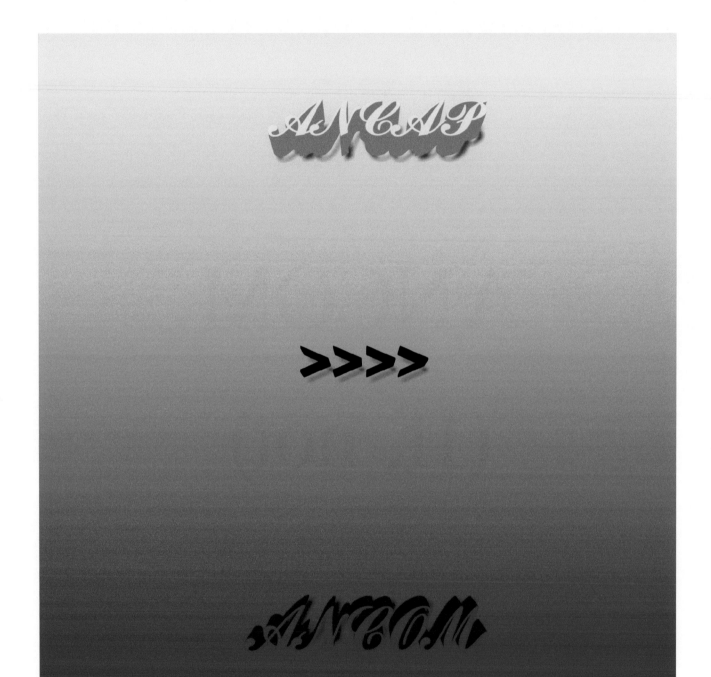

<u>Introduction</u>

What if the revolution didn't work as expected?

What if the revolution dies?

What if the revolt/revolution was crushed?

What if the proletariat never unites or remains less conscious?

What if all the proletarians perish?

What if human greed never ends?

What if anarcho-capitalists succeed in everything?

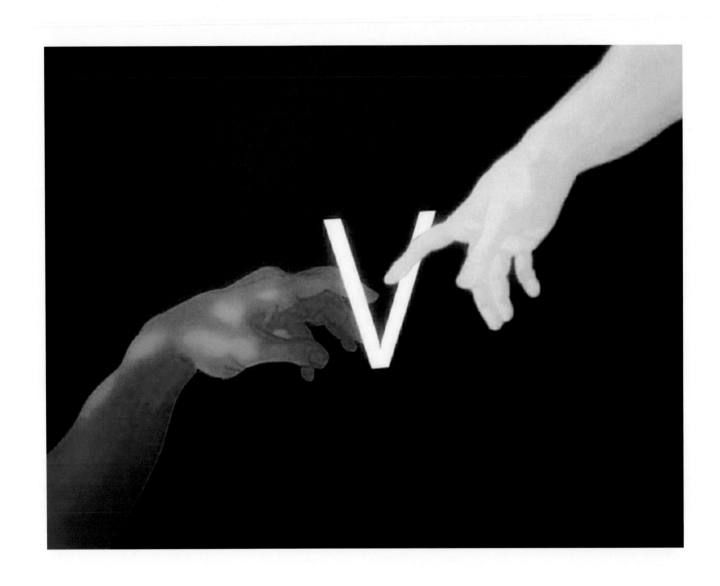

This photo is taken and altered from the creation of Adam. Here, the yellow hand, which is diagonally shown on the upper right, is for anarcho-capitalism. And the red hand, diagonally shown at the lower left, is for anarcho-communism. The white 'V' letter stands for voluntarism, while the black background represents anarchism (without governance).

Here, the yellow father hand transfers itself to socialist red society over time, through being intellectual, evolved, grown up, peaceful sapiens. During the 20th century alone, war murdered a huge number of people. Taxes and inflation have stolen more than all the wealth previously produced. The political lies, propaganda, and above all, education have twisted more minds than all superstitions of the past ever did.

Without reform or revolution, the ancient feudal society took on a new face, re-shaped, and called itself liberal. It lent a helping hand for feudal and mafia lords to cherish, with tolerance shown towards them by the government and the system to ensure everyone's greed is satisfied. But we poor beings, even though understanding that we can't satisfy our lust, know that our mind and society remained uncontrolled.

Even though there is enough to prove the badness of capitalism, people say they have an adjusting tendency. However, left to me, it looks like slavery. Free-minded thinkers and competitive people will easily reject a socialist society. Moreover, united proletarians are fake. It has never existed before. The reality is something like a lack of cooperation. Fakes, hate, cruelty, and selfishness exist within every people. So, the need of the hour is to have another kind of socialist society.

Socialism, a good dream, can be accomplished by every nation participating in it. That would be a good dream. Even if that occurs, the world under socialism will have a kind of capitalism within it. That's because people's wants and needs are different. For as long as money exists, so does capitalism.

Present and upcoming generations are still stuck in nationalism and religious issues. Let's hope that one day they may walk out of it.

But in the present world, people love their way of nationalism. Let them be like that. The want of the hour is not internationalism on the left line but worldwide national socialism. These nationalist commies will help us in creating a more peaceful, wealthy, and healthy citizen for future Ancap society.

As I already said, the world is moving towards anarcho-capitalist society through Agorism. As the black market and cryptocurrency are everywhere, this will reduce the state's power over time due to less taxation. And nowhere in history have people united or developed so much consciousness. It is rare that people have even started questioning the system and government. The want of socialism has reached a new zenith along with the rejection of authoritarianism.

So, what's next?

People are going to surrender socialism for liberty. That's right! Because they are not going to trust the leaders and leadership; instead, they acquire a self-leadership attitude. That's because the world is yet not a good place for communism, especially in one go.

So, that is what is mentioned by the illuminati about the new world order. According to that, a few million will survive. They will have an anarcho-capitalist society with voluntarism within them. This voluntarism, in later stages, will lead them to a new kind of agrarian society through a peaceful revolution. In fact, you can't call it a revolution. It will be a kind of peaceful, intellectual human who seeks evolution in their own will and way that which we can call anarcho-communism in nature.

Conclusion

Ancap society will have the kind of beings who may be regarded as Type 1 intelligent species.

Ancom society will be more advanced, and an outcome of voluntarism within Ancapitalism will be a Type 2 intelligent species, maybe a kind of immortal.

This Type 2 society will have an entirely different kind of species, and the system will be stateless, egalitarian, and moneyless. Indeed, a perfect utopia.

Soviet

Kerala

This kind of nationalist/regional commie will help create socially conscious people within a region - like what I have chosen, where people of a particular region should be taken into concern. Along with the pride of regional culture and heritage, we need to preach socialism within a society. And, over time, this kind of socialist education will help bring the rich and poor closer. It will also help to educate and bring unity, brotherhood, and peace to a certain degree. Not away nor against the present system. All they need is a leftist line of education. Other than socialism, nothing is going to bring permanent peace.

But not in one go!

UNITE

PEOPLE'S

ORGANIZATION - U.P.O

The proposed theory for alternate world order

What if we succeed in having another organization that works similarly, way more different, and better than the UN?

This flag is for United People's Organisation. This organization should work similarly to the UNO. The difference is that this should work for people's causes and not for nations.

The organization needs headquarters in a poor African country. It should also work and support in a manner opposite to the UN in every aspect.

Wherever the UN goes against the people, we would fight for the rights and needs of humans. Free the people and their will, their ways and work, for humanity, unlike the UN, which works entirely for nations' (masters') interests instead of the people's.

Even after it has been in existence for 70 years, the UN has failed to solve world problems. If it had been for humanity, the world would have been at peace within a few years of its birth. But just the UN flag has remained as the namesake of peace. Even by the name itself, it is clear it is representing nations and not people.So, what next? This should be a radical organization. It should run opposite/opposed to the UN. We must support every illegal, evil act and people, thus helping them establish and flourish rapidly. By adding them to the organization, their capital will help us a lot because no organization or foundation works without money and power. These illegal people, these criminals, and notorious gangsters will help bring the present system down, and the UN will get a competitor. Wc help those who favor and finance us – but only those who believe in, accept and agree with us. Only if there is no morality can we make the UPO a perfect competitor for the UNO.

The flag above represents every radical right and left with no exact motto or definition. This flag is for those who don't believe in the present system and those who seek rapid, radical change.

In short, to explain, we should never have exact mottos or preferences. In general, by hook and crook, we make this organization big enough to be a perfect competitor for the UN. This will help to wipe out people's belief in one kind of system, government, or organization and put an end to the monopoly of a particular organization or nation.

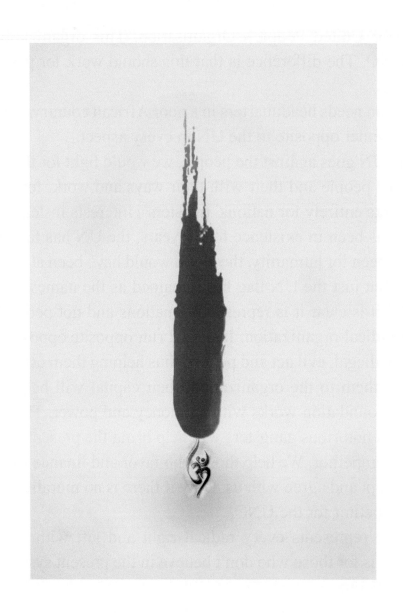

Hindu Bolsheviks

Proud nationalists.
The other kind of communists.
One who can identify and distinguish the difference between Bharath and India.
Patriotists with ultra-modern fascist mindset.
Usually well-dressed, strong-minded, lower class or
middle class Indian from forward caste family.

They are fans of right-wing parties.
They to believe in the hierarchy only if thou are at the top of the pyramid.

They emotionally and spiritually unite Hindus with Daliths, Sikhs, Jains,
Buddhists, Persians, Jews, Lingauiths. They can also encourage and help
be friendly with Muslims and Christians on the same national identity.

There is only one enemy to them. The one who speaks the truth that
hurts their imaginary identity or believes. They are here even before
independence, even before freedom struggle, even before Islamic
dynasties. Maybe their way of identity emerged in the vedic era of
division, hate, fear, cruelty, which they call Samskar(culture).

Why do I call them Hindu Bolsheviks instead of Hindu fascists or terrorists?

It's because they change their identity, point of view, words. According
to society's approach as well as people they interact with. For example,
if they are in business, deal with Muslims or Christians. Their way
of interaction will be different from the other right-wingers.

They cherished or created such a society; only blind by heart can accept it.
You are in private as well as in public sectors.
They are in the education, defense, science, medical
sector. In short, they are everywhere.

Calling them Bolsheviks has nothing to do with Marxism. Subconsciously they are
very conservative and traditional. Because of their belief in state and system with
authoritarian mindset, I felt a need to create another term for these hypocrites.

Sanskari fatale

Indian sanskari, savior of mother nature or Indian culture.

When the West and the Middle East try to end gloriest age-old dates back civilization and the next superpower of the world (India), they adopted psychological warfare.

In this war, women have much work and responsibilities.

As women are worshipped here from ancient time. They are also saviors and representatives of the culture.

Also, the virginity of women is precious because men are busied in earning. The cultural, religious concept is handled more importantly by the women.

As ascent is in love with jihad and convention thug, it's important to protect women and Dharma. Thus, women adopted or lived a lifestyle of orthodoxes. If these are sanskari women, then who is sanskari fatale?

They are some women within them who has a thing for spices.

They peek at men regardless of caste, religion, class.

Also, they will turn against the same man when things didn't go as expected or got exposed. Also, they use the feminist shield in times of crisis against men. Sadly this sadistic behavior won't help them against the woman. So, thou hate women whom they consider their competitors.

This actually made me believe that prostitutes are far better than these Fishes.

Patriotic minority

You are extremely amazing Patriots.

Most of their debate, discussion, social media platforms will be filled up with national anthem, national flag, Independence Day celebration, etc., with every national event and moment.

They are also immoderate fans of the India cricket team and other national sports.

Thou also show a high degree of respect, love, and support to regionalism and regional languages. Has great respect towards the Indian military and police department.

They are very rigid being's only reverence or fishing is that. They add thou religious concepts and symbols wherever they can.

Thus, my conclusion about them ends like this.

There is no such thing as moderate vs radical Islam. If they call themselves Muslims, then they are radical. As the war against Islam is almost all late, education is the only key to success.

People should be educated about Islam and its inner political agenda.

Printed in the United States
by Baker & Taylor Publisher Services